SONGS FROM THE DIRT

SECOND EDITION

LYRICS BY

JOSEPH NICKS

Published by Blue Jay Ink
Ojai, California
bluejayink.com

Book Design by Blue Jay Ink
Cover art by D. Reeser

This is MagPie Book #17. Visit our website (The Magnesium Pie Otherground) for lists of previous (and forthcoming) titles dating back to 1983.

For every single living thing
that's ever ceased its breathing ...

Songs From The Dirt, second edition

lyrics by Joseph Nicks

Album 1: *Reviver*

Album 2: *Scarlet-Hue Manatee*

Album 3: *Cursive Writing*
(I swear by these very words)

Thishit	2011	46
Wake Up For What??	2011	48
Bless My Solstice	2015	49
Forkin' Roads	2014	50
You	2015	51
Fluxup	2015	52
The Bulls	1984	54
Two	2009	60
Cracking Under The Wait	1991	62
Cyclosomatic	2014	64
At The End Of Today	2014	65

Album 4: *Thawless*

The Days Of Here And Now	2012	68
Homage	2010	70
By Bed Alone	2009	71
Blank Book	2004	72
Plumb Out Of Pipe Dreams	2014	74
These'll Be The Days	2015	76
Waiting For Spring's Recoil	2015	78
In The Bigendng	2015	80
Almost Everything I Think Of		
Breaks My Heart	2010	82
Why I Ride Alone	2014	84
The Last Days	1990	85
The Unsung Distance	2015	86

★already has music (13 of 48 titles)

REVIVER

The Grist Minstrels

As Long As I Can Run

been down on this bike, now
so damned many times
i'm surprised i still ride anymore

but as long as i can run
i fear i may run out of room
though i don't look for that
to happen soon

been down on these textbooks
so damned many times
i don't know what i know no more

but as long as i can think
i think i'll prob'ly think too much
which still somehow seems
nowhere near enough

      the new pain
      is really the old pain
      being felt on a whole 'nother plane

      the new world
      is really the old world
      with concrete poured over the ground

      and i got lost
      in the chorus
      while everyone else got so found

been down on my fathers
so damned many times
they've probably disowned me by now

but as long as i recall
it sets my head and heart to ache
and wishing we'd not make
the same mistakes

been down on these women
so damned many times
you'd think i'd have finally had my fill

but as long as i can dream
i'll prob'ly never get things done
and why would i just walk
if i could run

    the new pain
    is really the old pain
    being felt on a whole 'nother plane

    the new song's
    the same as the old song,
    new voices disguising the sound

    and i got lost
    in the chorus
    while everyone else got so found

A Color Undefined

i wish i were a color undefined;
a color yet to figure in,
so green and unfamiliar to their eyes

i wish i were a color still untried;
a color with no history,
no wavelength on the spectrum to belie;
a color all-encompassing
and swirling in the blackness and the white,
like melanin unblinded by the light

> yes, to break out of the black and white
> and join the colored people,
> intermingling our pigments
> 'til, too many to be labeled,
> we can't begin to think of one invalid,
> though unequal,
> embracing every earnest shade –
> i wonder if we're able

i wish i were a color seen anew;
a color with no forefathers
to taint the reputation of my hue;
a color not foreshadowing
nor lending any clue
as to the differences
we'll find in me and you

repeat refrain

These Are The Questions

"what?" is our urge
to identify stuff;
"who?" is no more
than a subset of "what?";
"where?" is our sense
of direction and depth;
"when?" is the distance
between now and then

"why?" is effect
in the search for a cause;
"which?" is the choice
in what isn't foregone;
"will?" is for tellers
of fortune and fame;
"won't?" is a negative
question of same

but "how?", the question bears weight
like each step upon the staircase:
it's how we know the process;
it is "why?" to the exposit

no, "how?" deserves some mention
alone among the questions
'cause "how?" allows each answer
to follow other answers,
outnumbering itself by n:1

Ouch

wherever there're winners,
there have to be losers –
it's just how the game is played;
wherever there's eating,
there have to be eaten –
that's the way this old world has been made;
as long as we're living, we're gonna keep dying
and loss only comes 'cause there's gain

    as long as you've already heard this before,
    it's hardly worth opening my mouth
    but as long as it keeps on hurting, my friend,
    the people will keep saying ouch

as long as suns come up,
suns have to go down –
i'm not the one writing the rules;
wherever belief is, there had to be doubt;
where warmth radiates, the source cools;
if you've finished building
what you hope to last,
you'd better hang on to your tools

    as much as we've been on this subject again,
    you'd think we'd have worn it all out
    but as long as it keeps on hurting,
    the people will keep saying ouch

as long as there's sex,
everyone's got to have it –
as long as they do, there'll be more;
as long as there's more,
there's bound to be less –
less room than the few had before;
as long as the burgeoning
squeezes the walls,
somebody will reach for the door

as long as new doors are revealed, at length,
there's some of us walking on out –
'cause as long as it keeps on hurting the people,
the people will keep saying ouch

You'll Have To Excuse Him,
He Was Accidentally Born

in my yearning adolescence
i could feel my unfelt essence
welling up to swell the chorus
with the silent effervescence
of those churning angstigated signs of life —
first life, like i could ever live
the way i knew we all could live
if life were left
to only lives and living things

in my learned convalescence
i could count the countless lessons —
all the novel things remembered on the way
to healing newfound feelings
that had long since gone astray
in the scratching, twitching, aching,
leaping wonders, heaven wonders
if it really does exist
while the promised land
recumbent at my feet
as their promises lie
helplessly down next to me
and mine — what's left of mine,
where i'm to whisper
indefinite words
as if to encourage,
endeafen its ears —
collective ears
of a latent public hearing
we had listened for
without a sound of ours

in my early obsolescence
i could see, too soon, senescence
handed down to my descendence
into life-saving forgetfulness
of how this wouldn't work
and couldn't –
maybe couldn't
though i couldn't cop to that
and that's exactly how i got here
'cause i couldn't cop to that –
in all my disbelieving
i would just as soon be leaving
with the colours and their bleeding
so as not to have to stand around
and watch all my believing
be leaving me behind

Whoa

whoa is me,
whoa is you,
whoa is when the whole wide world
got nothin' better to do
than to pull its reins on you

and i'm so full of whoa,
i can't even giddy-up no mo'

Lord, just a mule and forty acres —
that's all i ever asked of you;
well, this hard livin's made me so damned stubborn,
now i ain't gonna need that mule

'cause i'm so full of whoa,
i can't even giddy-up no mo'

now you can put me out to pasture —
you can strap me to the plow;
you can crack your whip across me
and i'll heave against the ground

but i'm so full of whoa,
i can't even giddy-up no mo'

everybody say, "hold your horses!"
but i been holdin' them so long,
i can't help but feelin' somehow
that it's doin' me some wrong
(if'n you get my meanin')

  yeah,
  whoa is me,
  whoa is you,
  whoa is when the whole wide world
  got nothin' better to do
  than to pull its reins on you

  and i'm so full of whoa,
  i can't even giddy-up no mo'

Waiting For The Sky To Fall

beyond the laughter
of the foolish spring;
the bronzing skin
of pleasured summer:

i've watched the days
surpass the years
and felt these feelings
growin' number

> look outside, the clouds have gathered
> to do what clouds are bound to do –
> another day won't see me waiting
> for the sodden sky to fall all over you

and, come the dry eyes
of the sober fall;
the longed-for lips
of sullen winter:

you'll see the day
when all my swollen hopes
of you no longer
even glimmer

> go inside, the sky has fallen –
> now there's nothing left to be
> but half of what we could've hoped for
> with the paths of two entwining you and me

The Plot

from the first time that i saw you,
couldn't think of nothin' else –
how the world can overwhelm your
all-consuming sense of self;
thinking far into the future,
when the one and one are two:
it can't help but be too long
'til i'm lyin' next to you

you know that each time that i see you,
something's stickin' in my craw:
that no matter how we struggle,
we're, none of us, above the law(s) –
there's just no way to avoid it;
there's just nothing we can do:
it can't help but be too long
'til i'm lyin' next to you

since that last time that i saw you,
can't keep my mind on much at all
and even after all this time,
i can't bring myself to bear the pall –
ah, but all too soon i'm comforted
to realize anew:
it can't help but be too long
'til i'm lyin' next to you

Hope On The Horizon

and back in the 18:00s;
the sun-weary sixes o'clock,
there wasn't much left
of the day or the life
to fuel my own flickering light

i lifted my head from my body,
gone leaden the length of the couch;
the shadows had slowly
enswallowed the room;
it seemed a long way to my feet

> there's hope on the horizon
> and i'm grasping for the thread;
> one minute i'll be dying
> and the next one i'll be dead

and back in the powder-blue darkness,
my eyes still trespass on the moon;
the same moon that's shone
on each present exchanged
for the mem'ries of long-greener pasts

i walk the deadly grey morning;
i can see what i've already seen,
my head so far above the cold earth,
it seems a long way to my feet

        "there's hope on the horizon",
        said the carrot to the stick,
        "a little faster and we'll be there",
        may just be life's cruelest trick

        "there's hope on the horizon",
        i was gasping for my breath;
        one minute i was dying
        and the next one i was dead

The Rookery

some will run,
some will fly,
some will lie still
where they are
upon an outsider's impertinent approach

still others remain there lifeless
until all trace of them subsides

but they all die...

Some Other Death

just want to watch them live –
just want to watch them out there
being alive

what a consanguineous feeling
to see life go on like that

but if you watch them long enough,
you'll see some other death

and if you watch each long enough,
you'll see another death

'Til You Go

i know that it's all goin'
and i know that this won't last;
i know that graves roll over
and that friends are fading fast

        i know it hurts to think, one day,
        our threads will come unsewn
        but i, for one, will still refuse
        to miss you 'til you go

i know the generations
leave an aching in our hearts;
i know that our togetherness
too soon becomes apart

        i know in our good-bying,
        we'll hear echoes of hello
        but i, for one, will still refuse
        to miss you 'til you go

i know we've all got ways to go
and things to do and say;
i know the weeks unravel us
and soon will come the day
when we stand chest to chest
before we turn and walk away

        i know there'll be a lot of things
        we'll wish that we had known
        but i, for one, will still refuse
        to miss you 'til you go

As Stupid As I Feel

and on the first day
of my prime,
i set right out
to right the world –
all too sure that
these ideals
weren't gonna get lost
in the swirl

       now years beyond those days have fallen
       all across these fallow grounds –
       if i was gonna get the calling,
       i'd have gotten it by now

       and my only consolation
       as my images unreel
       is that i probably don't look
       anywhere near
       as stupid as i feel
       as stupid as i feel
       as stupid as i feel

and on the last day
of the year,
i sat right down
to write the world –
all too swollen
with my problems
and all too long
gone un-girled

now hope can surge half-hearted
for a minute or an hour –
if she wasn't gonna call me,
i'm quite sure it would've been by now

and my only consolation
as the words and page congeal
is that it probably won't sound
anywhere near
as stupid as it feels
as stupid as it feels
as stupid as it feels

Epoch Eight Envisioned
(Pleistocene 2, Take 3)

lain low in the dark
that so long-prefigured light –
these are the nuts and bolts of life

come gather what's left
of nerve, muscle, breath and bone;
there's nothing else to call your own

though all you once lived for
has withered away with time
and it's gonna be a lonely climb

from out of the depths
where last-living relatives
lapsed into the infinitive

        come join The Heterozoic
        where life comes back to life –
        for every mass extinction,
        some genes are left unripe

        we write a new fossil record –
        dark horses brave new worlds;
        we're every mortal's next of kin –
        the double helix whirls

you "feel like you're dead",
but dead can no longer feel;
got to get back to what is real

come pick up what was, is,
was gonna be –
exhumed from your sleeping memory:

for all of the hopes and plans
of a lifetime spent,
most crashing down upon our heads;

not every idea has dawned
on the intellect;
some things have just not happened yet

      we can't help being ali-ive
      nor, too-soon, also dead
      and all that's yet to be written
      can't help remain unread

      we owe it to that which is given
      and, more, to just what gives
      to live as though we're still alive
      as long as we must live

      come join The Heterozoic
      where life comes back to life –
      for every mass extinction,
      some genes are left unripe

      we write a new fossil record –
      dark horses brave new worlds;
      we're every mortal's next of kin –
      the double helix whirls

SCARLET- HUE MANATEE

The Algernon - Gordon Effect

And If

i'm going down in the fields
where i saw my fathers go;
down in the fields
of the yes and maybe sow
all my new-mown expectations
where the roger waters flow

i'm going down in the fields
where i've watched the thistle grow
between my aching charlie gordon
and my edgar allen poems,
between my doubtful promised-landing
and revolving rubber soul

>   and if i've seen it once in thirty,
>   i'll be home by half-past due
>   and if there're four more years to find it,
>   i won't need the other two

i'm going down in the record books,
all simon-davies tuned,
from my hazy shade of winter
to my sunny afternoon

i'm going down on the road
tonight, at best, with half a clue;
down to the finish line,
so i can start anew

>   and if i, somehow, held the answers
>   at my wish and my command,
>   how could i hold them in the sweaty
>   palm of someone else's hand?

One-Wheel Drive (version 2)

from the outside of a city;
from the zoomed-out fish-eye gridwork
of a thousand open roads,

i can see my own dis-traction;
i can hear the empty thunder
of the thirsty dynamo

    now i know i've stayed too late
    into another wasted day,
    so grudgingly relinquishing its light
    to the life-sustaining onslaught of the night

from a mortgage and a pension;
from the inside of a prison
i've been building brick by brick,

i can feel the dissipation
of a lifetime's dogged straining
for that carrot on a stick

    and if i still have some motor
    when i get on out of here
    on two wheels and a tankful of tonight,
    gonna see if there's a story left to write…

Know Chance

and after all these eons,
still not a minute left to spare –
10,000 birds are flying,
9,000 more take to the air

for ev'ry one that fledges,
there's four times more don't leave the ground;
it's not unusual to lose you –
it's just good fortune to be found

        so put away your lucky charm,
        now, give your rabbit back his foot;
        if you could really come to know chance,
        you'd see luck does you no good

now, these boneyards yield such heirlooms,
who am i not to contemplate
all the evidence of each of
these not-so-simple twists of fate

for every one surviving
just long enough to go extinct,
the fraction fossilizing
are those of which we stop and think

        so just get over four-leaf clovers,
        give your rabbit back his foot;
        if you could really come to know chance,
        you'd see luck does you no good

you can walk under a ladder,
cross in the middle of the street –
do you really think it matters?
is there some fate that you can cheat?

no i wouldn't waste your breath, now,
blowin' all over your dice –
rolling sixes, sevens, eights
is gonna be your best advice

      your head's no better than your tail, boy,
      each lonely flip is on its own –
      try to prognosticate the outcome,
      might as well kiss the Blarney stone

Six Feet Down The Road (version 3)

when the long green season ended
and our labors were recalled,
we collected up our earnings
and stepped out into the fall

where the life comes back to living
and moves on to what comes next;
where a hundred highways beckon
those who've come to see what's left

    and, six feet down the road,
    we couldn't wait to round the bend –
    ten senses come unbound;
    two weary hearts were on the mend

    we walked all autumn-long
    and laid our heads where we saw fit,
    awake before the sun
    until the sky was long unlit

four-foot-two or two-foot-four,
we knew the nival times were nigh –
sure enough, we turned about to
look the winter in the eye

storm on storm, we had endured
out where the springtime feared to tread –
every March would find us workbound
down those vernal roads again

and so the seasons sailed —
we gladly followed them in kind;
i managed to forget
his years passed faster than did mine

he didn't wake one morning
just about a month ago
and now the time of year,
well i don't even care to know

there was such a lot to see yet —
there was so much left to say;
now the landscapes run together
and a day is just a day

not a home left to go back to,
no more family waits for me —
take a good long look around
next time you're hankering to be free

'cause you may find the time
but be forever out of place
and you may see the world
and, in it, never leave a trace:

i don't mean to stop living —
oh no, nothing of the sort
but six feet down the road
have up and left me four-foot short

so, two feet down the road,
i will recover all our tracks;
there may yet be a future
making peace with what has passed

Quitting Time?

i'm not the only one like me
who's overworked and underslept:
it's not so difficult to see
some have their rights, some get what's left

i've got a story yet to tell –
it's not like any one will hear;
i'd sooner keep it to myself
until that quitting time is near:

> here i am now, everybody –
> i ain't nothin' you ain't seen;
> got an ounce of fight left in me,
> feelin' beat down, feelin' mean
>
> no regrets about the space
> upon the line i didn't sign,
> but i'm wonderin' just how long
> before i call it quitting time

and so i wake up one more time,
pick up what little i've still got:
i've got a half a dozen friends
left i don't get to see a lot,

i've got a job that pays about as much
as it costs me to keep,
i've got a girl or two i think
of just before i go to sleep

repeat refrain

Endoscopic

if i think it,
have i thought it
knowing full-well i don't know?
can i possibly
be right if they
don't think it could be so?

> do i have to dye
> my skin transparent
> to show you what i'm made of?

if i say it,
need i say it
wired to a polygraph?
must my figures
all add up to
some purported aftermath?

> do i need a drink
> of bare-yum sulfate
> to show you what i'm made of?

must i notarize
the words i write
for them to be complete?
if i've felt what
can't be touched,
haven't my hands grown obsolete?

> do i have to cut
> myself wide open
> to show you what i'm made of?

When I Waste Out

when the last transmission trails off
and no further signal is received;
when not a spark transcends these gaps
and every muscle de-contracts;
when limbs and jaw go slack
and layer after layer falls away –
each tissue, in turn,
relinquishing its cellularity;

when the skeleton disaggregates,
far-flung across terrain
in random anonymity –
and even bone itself, so hard
and mightily defiant,
eventually succumbs
and crumbles into powder;

when all my former molecules
assume their new identities,
in time just as ephemeral as i was,
or any mountain, ocean, atmosphere;

will any rock be left unmolten?

will any sea stretch unevaporate?

will any air escape its own rarefaction?

will any consciousness remain
to contemplate how substance
subjugates all fleeting structure?

By Bread Alone?

it's hard to think there's more to life
than just these beans and cheese and rice
when you're no more than hungry
and all the world grows ugly

it's hard to think of anything
more worth the pain of gathering
throughout all of Pangaea,
enwrapped in a tortilla

all science and philosophy,
all art and high technology
can't from starvation hide us
with no chilés alongside us

My Dying Birthplace

i'm leaving you now,
my dying birthplace;
your summer and your people
and your green
and, never coming back
for your duration,
i'll watch you turn
and wither in my dreams

you waved me wayward,
wind-driven, destitute
with all the world unwalked
beneath my feet;
ink-starved and compassless,
blank-booked and threadbare-backed –
eyes on horizons
that were decades deep

   i turned to catch the drift of it
   for one last time before the driven snow
   obscured the trails that wound around
   the everything that everyone should know

   somehow i wasn't quick enough
   to put it all together way back then,
   but everything i understand
   has rolled its long slow way through where i've been

come now to lay me down
back on my birthing grounds;
we knew it'd have to happen
one fine year;
walking my last days out,
untangling hopes and doubts,
looking for no more than to
weigh them here

i've made my peace with you,
my dying birthplace;
who'll be the first to goin' –
me or you?
guess we'll be finding out
'fore too much longer, now –
they got to plow these fields
to make more room

All Believing Needs Be Leaving

in the twilight, now is nigh night
and the shadow of a doubt
looms larger in the landscape
than it ever has before,
bespeaking this nocturne of tide –
rising, even as it deepens
to swamp these last few glimmers
of unguarded gullibility
the day has steeped us in...

This Song Is Not For Long

this song is my nervous breakdown
this song is my suicide note
this song is me "going postal"
this song is my last lifeboat

this song is my self-surrender,
my white and my checkered flag
this song is the infrastructure
i'm feeling begin to sag

      and what's gonna save me
      is not a thing, save me –
      if i can't get over
      the wall to October,
      i guess i weren't meant to;
      so i'd better tend to
      those last-minute details
      before the next ship sails

this song is my anesthesia,
the blanket on my deathbed
this song is my fifth dementia,
retreating inside my head

this song is my court appearance,
my final "not guilty" plea
this song is my valid passport,
my ticket to Willoughby

      the snow it comes swirling,
      i'm going with Rod Serling
      and, Mr. E. A. Poe,
      his stories'll be stowed
      somewhere in my conscience
      'tween Judas and Pontius,
      the sober and caustic,
      disheartened, agnostic...

CURSIVE WRITING

(I swear by these very words)

BOOMSLaNg

Thishit

morning traffic swells the highways,
sea of brake lights in the dark –
for as fast as wheels are rollin'
we might just as well be parked

prophets tell us how we're gonna
have to do more now with less –
no one sees them lift a finger,
pull their weight like all the rest

> shit's not funny anymore,
> as if it ever really was:
> "every dog will have his day"
> but no one down here ever does

makin' hundreds, it costs thousands
on the easy payment plan;
all this time we trade for money
slippin' through our hands like sand

but your vote is your salvation,
smell of change is in the air:
choose prosperity or freedom,
master of your own despair

> shit's not funny anymore,
> as if it ever really was:
> the way they amplify each broadcast,
> loud as mumbles, clear as fuzz

gonna baby all these babies –
ain't no child left behind
'til they're eighteen and they're legal,
then we'll make 'em do their time

sell your soul to our dish network,
turn your brain to microsoft,
plug your i-pod, ear-pod, nose-pod,
feed your facebook, twitter twat

> shit's not funny anymore,
> as if it ever really was:
> long-awaited, slicker version
> new.0 is all the buzz

high-and-might-evangelizers
tell us when the world will end:
once you die, you'll live forever –
we get ten percent 'til then

got to lay your body down
before another mornin' comes,
while the workless, free-lunch loafers
make your sleep come all undone

> shit's not funny anymore,
> as if it ever really was:
> why should you listen to the "why"s
> when you can give us your "because"

Wake Up For What??

wake up, your fortune to amass –
wake up to take it up the ass;
another year, you can retire,
give your regards to those enmired,
still, in the cesspool of success:
float to the top and be the best

> let's go lose a little more,
> let's get down closer to the floor,
> see how long we have to wait
> for these last years to seal our fate

you stagger through your working day
on flimsy promises and pay;
go where you can to find your sleep –
it won't be long, it won't be deep
and, should you die before you wake,
the state will carve up your "estate"

> *repeat refrain*

i had a dream still packed away –
i pulled it out one rainy day
only to find it had expired,
no further action was required;
i drove downtown to have a drink,
wait for the sorry sun to sink

> *repeat refrain*

Bless My Solstice

and on this post-paternal Father's Day —
about four-and-a-half A. D.,
everybody's basking
in the overcast mass-stranding
of life's turgid played-out play

handed down and run aground
like gas upon the water
or the smell of barbecue;
another half a dozen hallmarks
and a champagne-guzzling brunch

and on the longest, widest day
of another drawn-out year,
the father's going on again —
the sun is standing still

Forkin' Roads

i remember when i wrote that –
and i admit i still feel more-or-less that way;
i just keep it to myself now –
'cause what you think,
well you don't ever have to say;
if i really had a mind to,
anyway, i'd say it differently these days

i remember when i worked there
and it's not that i regret those labored years;
but i didn't trade my best days
for a pension and a bellyful of beer;
there's some distance yet to go now –
i'm still gonna have to shift a couple gears

> forkin' roads;
> forkin' roads;
> i've been sailin' all along
> these forkin' roads
> and my good old friends
> been leavin' me in droves
>
> and they're not the only ones –
> seems me and every who i was
> got separated
> at each forkin' of the road

i remember when we said it –
it was true then, and it's even truer now;
but for every bifurcation,
re-convergence isn't always disallowed;
if we somehow have a mind to,
we can count all that we've lost among the found

> *repeat refrain*

You

are every mile of road
that you have travelled;
every decent book
you've ever read

are everyone you've made
authentic love to;
every song that made
you sing along

are every bleak expanse
you've gotten used to;
every dead-end job
at which you've toiled

are every utterance
you have atoned for;
every honest blunder
you have made

are every fist you've swung
at your tormentors;
every earnest question
you've put forth

are every fervent cause
that you have championed;
each shadow of a doubt
you've entertained

Fluxup

took a walk down
through the decades
to a place i used to know,
that i could swear i only left
a couple neighborhoods ago

which of us has changed more
is the question of the hour –
and i'd lay you even odds:

because, for each familiar landmark
long since plowed beneath these streets,
still stands a place i knew so long ago –
and i remember how it looked
through these same eyes,
long before they saw all they've since seen

and all the distant worries
that plagued me as a kid
have come to their collision
in technicolor slo-mo,
swirling all around
my helpless front-row seat

but all these literati,
well they've got no time for that –
no time to hear it, understand it,
let it get under their skin

they've got a million manuscripts to read,
a raft of new reviews to write,
a social order to maintain

while a surging river of verse
flows silently some feet beneath their feet –
denim dripped in blood and sweat
and alcohol and debt;
hours flown to days to years
and years back to the dirt

The Bulls

I

Hear the laughter of the bulls –
    younger bulls
What a joyous, youthful world into which,
    listeners, it lulls
As they strain their ears to hear
    the something(s) once they heard so plain
While the memory's forgotten
Of recesses they were not in
    and the blubbering, in vain,
    When the boys, boys, boys
Began to make their manly noise
To the tender underbellies slammed
    against by fists clenched full,
    Of the bulls, bulls, bulls, bulls,
        bulls, bulls, bulls
On the playgrounds of the sissies and the bulls

II

Hear the dictum of the bulls –
      louder bulls
What a rich new world of knowledge
      over which their lecture mulls
As they tell us, tell us, tell us
Of the wisdom they'll impart
And they sell us, overzealous,
On the truth they tell, in part
      While our queries to their theories
Of what's wrong and right and left,
      Painted pictures in a series
On our dumbstruck palettes cleft,
      Are the silly
      Questions left,
      Questions cut
Down to size in our eyes
Over which they pull the wool,
      the blinding, scratching, sniffling wool
      of the bulls, bulls, bulls, bulls,
          bulls, bulls, bulls
In the teaching and the preaching of the bulls

III

Hear the roaring of the bulls –
       bulls in charge
What a repertoire of orders:
       lift that bale! tote that barge!
In and out the flaming hoops
       we jump through
       oh what splendid tricks we do
To the cracking of the whip
And no one gives the master lip
       Oh what brains
       Oh what balls
In the shots the foremen call
       to the aftermen behind them
       and below them, at their best
To the backs that break beneath them
       Just to earn a day of rest
       Oh the burning in the breast
Of those who say "yes sir" in jest

Such a test of manly will
    To shrug it off and linger still
As they deride, ride, ride
All up and down our bruised backsides
        Each chance to think
        Never think
You know you don't get paid to think
And that's all you need to know
        I'll tell you all you need to know
        When I think you need to know it
        If you remember, never show it
What I tell you will be different every time
Just the opposite of what you thought this time
        Until the mind it dims and dulls
        Each new order it annuls
In the boring down of bulls
    Of the bulls, bulls, bulls, bulls,
            bulls, bulls, bulls
In the roaring and the goring of the bulls

IV

Hear the wails of the bulls –
    prowling bulls
While the world's kept safe at night
By the cruising black-and-whites
    Riding heard upon the town
And surrounding countryside
Where I've found a place to hide
    And climbed inside
Giving berth to further fears
    Drawing near
    In the distance that I hear
    So far and wide
Growing narrower and nearer steadily
In a distance I would give up readily
    So much larger when it's there
    In the magnifying air
So much bigger than a car
And but one or two, there are,
    To inquire as to the nature
    Of that held suspect in the night
When here they were, I was sure
In my answers, was secure
    And responding in a way
Above suspicion
A renewal of conviction
That it was not for a crime
    That I had run
    Nor a gun
Just the conscience of a guilt
That I had won
What a singleness of purpose
    Having only
    scratched the surface
    Of a question
They'd not sense enough to ask

But to bask in bright
Spotlight, my hands held high
      Into the night,
      Explaining to their
      Waning disbelief
What a relief it is, I'd say,
Not to have to hide away
To come out and show
my face in a clear and open space
      Of white midday
      Perhaps they'd let me go
      (or take me) far away
And not another night to pray
That I can hold the bulls at bay,
Escape to lie down one more day
      Where now-extinct and weary wolves
      Used to lie in wait for bulls
For the cunning of the bulls
For the running of the bulls
Like a sniper under fire of the bulls
      Impeding the stampeding of the bulls
      Through the choking
Undergrowth of the silenced bellowthroats
      of the bulls, bulls, bulls, bulls,
            bulls, bulls, bulls
To the silence in the minus of the bulls

Two

i'm not tryin' to be your one and only;
i have no design to make you mine –
i'm just sayin' some day's bound to be lonely
an' i'd be so inclined to share your time

i have longed to make your sweet acquaintance;
i've been scared to death i might succeed
and, though it feels so right to be around you,
i know no one needs to be in need

    two is such a funny little number –
    it can only be made up of one and one;
    the smallest way to be part of a plural
    is to keep it just between and not among

i'd like to say i'll always be there for you
but i can't guarantee how long i'll live
and all these things i now so freely give you,
i may not always be equipped to give

anyone can pledge unflagged allegiance;
everyone will say they'll never leave:
how can we be sure what fate awaits us –
how long will it be 'til we'll be grieved?

    two's a much sought-after little number,
    as elusive as those many times its size –
    how often do you think it actually happens
    that the two don't somehow,
    somewhen come untied?

it's been so long since we have looked around us
and even longer since we've ventured there –
we can't just keep ourselves stuffed up inside us,
ensmothered by the same old stale air

you can't be sore at every girl i talk to;
i can't get mad 'cause you make some guys hard –
if we can't take our eyes off of each other,
monogamy can only go so far

two is such a claustrophobic number –
there are times it doesn't have much up on one;
the quickest way to breed dissatisfaction
is to keep it just between and not among

Cracking Under The Wait

well i thought about women
for twenty-six years
and, when it came time to explore,
i picked myself up,
took a walk 'round the block
and sat down, thought about them some more

i got quite a few things
on my mind, little child;
a couple of them belonging to you,
but your family won't want to hear
nothing like that –
anyway that's not anything new

> don't think that i don't think
> about you that way
> and don't think that i'm being terse;
> sure, i'd like to get into
> your pants, little one,
> but i've got to get out of mine first

well i thought about living
for seventeen years,
'bout dyin' for seventeen more
but before i could live,
much less die, like i should,
one grey day i woke up thirty-four

i got nearly enough things
to keep my brain booked
'til two thousand seventy-three
but i guess i got 3-4
degrees more to get
'fore they'll take much of this seriously

don't think that we haven't
got time left to kill –
don't think we don't drive our own hearse;
yes, i'd love to get into
your pants, little girl,
but i've got to get out of mine first

well i thought about ways which
the world might go 'round
if it didn't go 'round like it does,
and just when i thought
that i had me a plan,
was it "why"s to become a "because"?

got a pain in the pain
that pains me
'til i can't say "ouch" no more,
so instead i say
six thousand things
i think nobody's said before

don't think i'm not trickling
out of myself;
don't think i don't have wounds to nurse;
i'd just love to get into
your pants, little one,
but i've got to get out of mine first

Cyclosomatic

the summer you
has gone to seed –
its limbs so heav'ly-laden
with fruit so ripe and thick
and cracking in the heat,
that its melting juices
flow all down your trunk

the autumn you
takes stock of every tissue,
counting off each color in its kind –
swirling out
to take the wind
in equilíbrium

the winter you
is lean and taut,
has got back down to wood
that sways so unencumbered in the air,
and goes about its business –
the paring down,
the winnowing
of anything excess
that impedes the efflorescence
of the all-too-soon-consummered
vernal you

At The End Of Today

at one end of today
lies what's coming –
cleverly creeping unnoticed on by
your every intentional vigil –
inevitably while you lie sleeping,
tomorrow turns into today

at today's other end
lies what has been –
swear it was just here
a moment ago,
all evidence points to that fact –
as soon as you snooze in your newness,
it slyly slips out the back door

at the end of today
lies your epitaph –
all of the yesterdays
you really were
and all the tomorrows
you would be

THAWLESS

THE ICE SAGES

The Days Of Here And Now

and on the verge of nothingness,
i made myself a vow:
that all the bloody howling
i have carried so deep down
would somehow spill out onto these,
the days of here and now

i swear it by my aching back,
the furrows of my brow:
the dead are as alive as all
the living will allow
in spite of slowly dying in
the days of here and now

      none know what's coming
      and all know what's gone –
      the question still remains,
      "is there life beneath the lawn?"
      and all the research shows the things
      the research hasn't shown:
      though we may breathe collectively,
      each breath expires alone

reverberating echoes
of the silence come aloud;
by the time you have the time, you find
your time's all but run out –
you scramble to take stock of all
the days of here and now

recounting all the chapters,
steeped in adjectives and nouns
of all you have belabored,
all you've failed to put down –
the verbs have all gone verbal
'til the days of here and now

      death to the future
      and birth to the past,
      today's about as long
      as this living's gonna last
      and all the lies i've told myself
      to keep myself alive
      have grown so much less likelier
      than biblically contrived

attended by the lonely drone
of engines fueled by doubt;
forebodings off the starboard bow,
a bilgeful of regret,
i steam the naked, nervous, numbered
days of here and now

Homage

i think of Archimedes
every time i screw
the cap off of a bottle
or i torque these bolts anew

i think of Nick Copernicus
'n' up the sun
gone down with every nightfall,
though it's just the Earth that's spun

        and then i think of Alfred Weg'ner,
        smile as plate slides under plate –
        i watch the rising of dishwater
        as i contemplate our fate

i think of dear old Darwin,
watch it all unfold
in shale upon the sandstone –
greatest story ever told

i think of Gregor Mendel,
generations waived;
to give the rest a chance, i'll
wear these genes down to my grave

        and then i think of Rachel Carson
        as i tune my ears for spring
        and though i scarcely hear a flutter,
        guess we'll see what summer brings...

By Bed Alone

i have learned not to be learned
and i know, now, not to know
but can't think how i'd stop thinking
how much thinking's left to go

    if confusion is the road to understanding,
    i can tell you i've been long years on the way
    ah, but few roads end at given destinations;
    when i'll understand enough, i cannot say

i've been angered by their anger
and i fear i've lost my fear
but i'm too sad to trade this sadness
for just crying in my beer

    if i'd felt everything there was to be feeling,
    would some anger, fear, or sadness have escaped?
    and if happiness were something i aspired to,
    could i feel it, having felt no other way?

i have worked out how to work this,
sweat of brow for daily bread
but i have always felt encumbered
any place i've lain my head

    if i stopped to lay me down ev'ry so often
    and find temporary refuge in this sleep,
    would the day not come when i'd succumb forever,
    find the climb back out of it a bit too steep?

Blank Book

in the colder rooms of downtown
where the not-so-heated dwell,
you can tune in to the tick-and-talk
of nothing left to tell

or escape into the sadness
of past hopes and future fears;
you can stay for one more hour,
one more week or one more year

> but i can take you out there
> to the dark end of the light
> where you can see beyond
> the shiny edges of the night,
> unsteeped in these imaginings
> of blindness and insight

in the fathomless expanses
sprawled between the books and shelf
where nobody has to teach you
how to be all by yourself:

you can live the lengths of lifetimes;
you can die a thousand deaths;
you can weigh upon their thinking;
you can linger in their breath

> but i can take you deeper
> than what's never been before;
> i can find the places
> everybody else ignored;
> i can show you to yourself,
> just down this corridor

in the paperless existence
of the ages gone before,
when the lonely words-of-mouth
had to amount to so much more

than the sum of everything that
has been ever written down;
we'll never know what's blown away with
little hope of being re-found

       but i can take you down
       into the basements of back then;
       i can take you up
       into the attics of again –
       far beyond the archives
       of a given where or when

Plumb Out Of Pipe Dreams

maybe i'll work hard enough,
make foreman one fine day
and maybe make them listen to
what workers have to say

maybe we can have a hand
in setting these things right;
maybe we can win the war
by giving up the fight

       but i don't look to find salvation
       in the chances of a chance –
       no i don't want to get caught up in
       the perhapsedness of that

maybe soon i'll understand
how all this shit works out;
maybe you'll illuminate
each shadow of my doubt

maybe i can find a way
to make you cut the crap
and learn again to navigate
without your two-bit maps

    repeat refrain

maybe i'll get back to feel
not always so fucked-up;
maybe i'll convince myself
i've finally had enough

maybe i'll give in and start
believing once again;
maybe it will be cool
to be what we've always been

repeat refrain

These'll Be The Days

those were the days —
no doubt about it,
and they'll never
be again,
but did we really
try to live them
for their time and
in their time —
or were we mired in
our nostalgia
or caught up in
days to come?

       'cause these'll be the days,
       i'm tellin' you right now-ow
       no need to look for rays
       of new-dawning tomorrows

       yeah, these'll be the days,
       reminisced in joy and sorrow,
       we'll long be longing for
       in the brave new days to follow

we could just lie
about good-bying
our eternal
heaven-scent
but 'til we lie
down to our dying
still's a chance to
make amends;
we've had a good
run, no denying,
though they ain't seen
nothin' yet

repeat refrain

Waiting For Spring's Recoil

was a time you felt it plainly
when you lived out in the air
where the wind comes at you sideways
and the rain down from above;
a roof, a couple walls can do so much

but there's something there inside you
that defies both space and time;
when it comes, it comes to creeping
in between what's yours and mine –
it's strange how you can feel what you can't touch

was a time you saw it clearly
from a precipice or two;
now the climbing's not so easy,
though there's not much else to do –
you wonder when you'll see you've seen enough

now the sun comes up so early
and the day goes on so long –
it's so pregnant with rememb'rance
of those lives both come and gone;
it's hard to realize you've gone so soft

and you may not want to know it
after all these spun-out years,
how each night you drowned your thinking
with a half a dozen beers
that weren't enough to buy your conscience off

yeah, you know you must get on with it –
today won't be too soon
so you gather up your blueprints
as you wander room to room
and six clocks all agree it's six o'clock

In The Bigending

there's for sure
enough for ev'ry –
body 'til
there isn't anymore –
there'll be less
to worry about
tomorrow than
there was the day before

> lookin' around you,
> there's way more to it
> than the end of you and me –
> in the bigending,
> it should be eas-yer
> than it's always tried to be

we can reap
the fruits of others'
labor while
our own seeds come unsown –
we can keep
on pushin' on
to nowhere 'til
there's nowhere left to go

> *repeat refrain*

to the earth
i now commend
the endermost
of all i've ever been –
if i've lived,
i've lived to breathe
their final breath,
my fathers' last of kin

repeat refrain

Almost Everything I Think Of Breaks My Heart

in a land across the land
i've heard so many speak in awe of
lies a place to quench our soles
and send us marching on undaunted:

  i've plainly felt so many
  things i couldn't wrap my hands around
  and each and ev'ry evening
  beckons me with sight and scent and sound

    but before i can partake of
    any breath it will impart:
    almost all the roads i trav'll come unraveled –
    almost everything i think of breaks my heart

from a book among the books
of everything i can remember,
having plumbed the depths long nights
'til my own thinking came untethered:

  i thought about the many
  things i knew too well i didn't know
  and wished i could be more like
  those whose thinking must be surely so

    but one thing i must remember
    every time i crave their smarts:
    almost everything i feel wrinkles my thinking –
    almost everything i think of breaks my heart

in a room within a room
where they are mingling all around me,
there's so much that i can't touch
and feel the distance so profoundly:

we all talk about the many
things that there must be to talk about –
then her eyes and mine entwine,
guerrilla-wise in shadows of a doubt

but there's something to consider
now before we even start:
almost all i can imagine ends entragened –
almost everything i think of breaks my heart

Why I Ride Alone

you can't help it you're so damned cool –
i can't help it if i don't care that i'm not;
but i'll tell you what i can help:
feeling sold-out for those things i've never bought

you can't blame a dog for dying –
you can't blame me for refusing to forget;
but the blame lies in denying
all the life around you just becomes more death

      and that is why i ride alone
      into the darkness of these roads
      without a lover or a friend
      who'll be beside me without end –
      another road runs headlong into
      yet another road and then
      i watch the purple sky collide
      with some-ten-thousandth fool sunrise

it's not my fault that i love you –
it's sure not your fault you're not in love with me;
where the fault is is in hoping,
hov'ring round here as if you might someday be

      repeat refrain

The Last Days

don't need to be so sad
because we've reached our apogee;
i won't be here, come summer
but somebody else will be

and you, you've got some days
before you see the last of me,
i wouldn't want "good bye"
to dominate our glossary

   these are the churning days of which
   our dreams will soon be made;
   the days of clarity in retrospect
   we'll laugh at one fine day;
   the dizzy days and nights of lifetimes
   finally gotten underway

and so we go away,
there're still some places left, at that;
a long time now, you must've known
the last days couldn't last

they'll soon turn into other days,
the first of which we'll miss
and if we haven't learned a thing or two,
they could be worse than this

   these are the days of dying/hope
   of days that dawn anew,
   the days of finding out, in fact,
   if days are numbered too
   and, these, the days of passage,
   make us wonder but for whom

The Unsung Distance

the answer to the question
always seems to be, "don't ask" –
no time for contemplation
when you're trading facts for facts

attempting to discuss it
only leads to reprimand
but, if you're not confused,
how will you ever understand?

        you gaze out across the lecture hall
        at all there is to "know" –
        it's gonna be a long, slow row to hoe

the humanest condition,
last two centuries, i'd say,
has to do with nothing more than
workers trading days for pay

and, breathed between these weekends
and a measly couple beers:
"if I can only make it
just another fifteen years"

        hear it all throughout the factory,
        the workdays come and go –
        it's gonna be a long, slow row to hoe

but walked along those long hauls
and gone down their crippled stares,
enlightened by their windows
and then out into the air

a moment still belongs to you
nobody else can claim —
you've lost your train of thought again,
it's such a goddam shame

      walking stooped into this builderness
      where nothing seems to grow —
      it's gonna be a long, slow row to hoe

www.ingramcontent.com/pod-product-compliance
Lightning Source LLC
Chambersburg PA
CBHW051637050426
42443CB00025B/431